GW01463878

OUT OF MY SYSTEM

Brian Donovan Thompson was born in New Zealand in 1932.

The family returned to Ireland in 1939 following the death of his grandmother.

The last war disrupted his childhood and he went to school in Belfast, Donegal, Derry and Dublin before emigrating to England in 1951.

He joined the British Army and in 1957 was demobilised in London, where he worked for an insurance company before leaving to run his own business at the age of 28.

He taught himself how to restore old houses and eventually purchased and restored seventy historic buildings in four countries. These properties included two English manor houses, two Irish castles and forty-one Hudson River mansions in New York State.

Brian now lives with his wife Elyse in Cloghan Castle, Banagher, which they open to the public every summer.

Brian Donovan Thompson

OUT OF MY SYSTEM

An Assortment of Pithy Poems

with a
Foreword by Malcolm Ross-Macdonald

Illustrated by Rosalind Fanning

Battlements Press
2000 AD

Set in 12 on 13–15 point ITC Galliard
to Royal 8vo
by Richard Graham for

BATTLEMENTS PRESS
Lusmagh, Banagher, Co Offaly
Republic of Ireland
tel/fax: +353 509 51650

A catalogue record for this title
is available from the British Library.

ISBN 0-9538463-0-X

Published by
BATTLEMENTS PRESS
Lusmagh, Banagher, Co Offaly
Republic of Ireland
and
Printed in Great Britain
by Antony Rowe Ltd., Chippenham, Wilts.

Contents

Author's Note

I have found that a good way to get rid of pent-up
feelings is to sit down and write a poem. It gets it
'out of my system'. The knack of trying to make the
words rhyme is another diversion, and I like a poem
with hidden little barbs and a sting in the tail.
Sometimes my poems would go out in attempts to
draw attention to problems that were unlikely to be
received sympathetically in an ordinary letter, and
the recipients responded in like fashion.
My wife and daughter Rosalind have, for years,
been saving these doggerels and encouraged me to
have them published, so here they are.

B.D.T.
Cloghan Castle
May, 2000

Foreword

THOSE of us who were privileged to attend the wedding breakfast of Catherine at Cloghan Castle will – whatever other memories we may have of the occasion – have carried away one that remains incredible: of Brian reciting a poem he had composed to celebrate one of Catherine's many endearing characteristics. That and the gales of laughter which followed its concluding line. (Those who had the misfortune to be absent that night will now be able to catch up on the joke, for the poem is printed on page 34.) Like me, many will have wondered that such a comic talent could be contented with the fleeting applause of the after-dinner recital.

Wonder no more. For here is a veritable bouquet of comic blossoms from the same pen, each (if I may mix my metaphor until it is thoroughly Irish) a gem in its own right. This may be read with many a titter but never a blush; and, in reading on, each will become the favourite of *some* reader, though I doubt any two will agree. And that, when you consider it, is the strength of the collection as a whole – there is something here for everyone.

The nostalgic will like *the Emergency* or *Belfast Blitz*. The convalescent will warm to *Hospital*. The lover of pure comedy could hardly do better than *Socks* or *Drive-in Movie* or *The Bed*. And, though the collection forms a single, organic whole, the extraordinary complexity of Brian's own character is, I think, best revealed in, on the one hand, *The Ferry,* and, on the other, *Living in My Castle,* with *For Elyse – the Girl in Blue* in between. My own favourites? *The Parachutist* (which probably shows my age) and *Female Teenager, 1999* (which probably shows that I still have some growing up to do).

Read, enjoy, and – as with all the best organic produce – pick your own!

Malcolm Ross-Macdonald
Banagher – *February 2000*

Living in My Castle

I climb the spiral staircase
Some ancients made of stone,
And from the battlements look down
  In sunlight - on my own.

I see the sparkling waters,
  The lake from Shannon's shore,
That stretches from our castle
  For seven miles and more.

I hear the geese a honking,
  White swans beneath me glide
And forty thousand wild birds
  Find this a place to hide.

I walk down to the Court Room,
  With oak beams up on high,
The brooding silence reeks of power,
  And strangers wonder why.

I pass the chamber haunted
  By many hacked alive,
When fighting off the English,
  In fifteen ninety-five.

I walk the narrow passageway
  And might perchance to trip,
Our ghostly old retainer,
  Likes to give us all a flip.

B.D. THOMPSON

I sit down in the drawing room
  And look at panelled walls,
Round deep set old embrasures,
  The past just calls and calls.

I know that others sat here,
  Who talked by candlelight,
Of shipwrecks and past battles
  In the middle of the night.

I know I cannot stay here,
  One has to leave or die,
But I have loved and lived here,
  For years gone swiftly by.

At night with log fires burning
  In Main guard's huge old grate
And candles lighting ancient walls,
  Good food upon my plate.

My family gathered round me,
  Contented and replete,
We toast the spirits of the past
Whilst standing on our feet.

My wife made this home beautiful,
  With love and care and taste.
If she were not the heart of it,
  The rest would all be waste.

How many dogs have lived here?
  How many cats were born,
To hunt the mice and chase the birds,
  From twilight dusk to dawn?

I look out on the parkland,
  With happy grazing sheep.
The badgers snuffle round for worms,
  When night owls do not sleep.

I rebuilt all the battlements
  Blown off by cannon balls.
It took three men six years of work
  To rebuild circle walls.

I planted many oak trees,
  Full thousand seventy-five,
Put paintings rare on inside walls
  And brought the place alive.

Yes – I have loved to live here,
  Its visions and its smells,
With space and peace and beauty,
  To cast their timeless spells.

So many here before me,
  The future may be fine,
But let me have a few more years,
  To say, "You're mine, you're mine."

I'm only here a short life span,
  But I have done my best,
To leave the castle much improved
  When I am laid to rest.

It has been said that anybody crazy enough to consider it important to winch up 150 truck loads of stones to rebuild the battlements ninety feet in the sky is *really seriously crazy*. So if you do not like the poems – blame it all on the battlements!

Our 1,500 acres of shooting rights are now a wildlife sanctuary.

Celtic Tiger

I love a good tribunal,
  With builders in their shoals,
Tall tales of lots of money
  For officials with a Rolls.

With paper bags of unmarked punts,
  To give to a T.D.
For Party funds and other needs,
  But not for you or me.

They gave it all for nothing,
  'A thank you or a smile'.
As millions wafted round the State
  And Haughey lived in style.

There's nothing like a clean clean shirt,
  Or one that's made in France.
Yes – keeping up one's image,
  Just cannot rest on chance.

A golden happy circle,
  All coming down with cash,
Pass round the information
  And make more loot to stash.

True purpose of Tribunals,
  Is to cause a long delay
And bring knowing smiles to lawyers,
  Who net thousands every day.

The Emergency

WHEN I was a lad in Donegal,
  We could not get white bread at all.
The ration of tea was very small,
  But we had lots of butter.

In Derry, Belfast and Coleraine,
They used to search for eggs in vain,
In England it was just the same,
  They really had no butter.

The Second World War was a frightful chore,
  With hellish hardship planned.
But we sat tight, well out of the fight,
  In our neutral well-fed land.

Great nations fought with a single thought,
  To win against the foe,
In Ireland we just ate our sweets,
  We didn't want to know.

I once asked why we did not try,
  To set poor Europe free,
But I was bid to close my lid,
  In this *Emergency*.

They crowded us on the Swilly 'bus,
  We could not have a car.
But I liked best, the odd request,
  To smuggle near and far.

We all then made cross border trade,
  Exchange was our endeavour,
On another slant, without much cant,
  We all thought smuggling clever.

[13]

We did it both by day and night,
By methods devious and bright,
Tea for butter cash for bread,
A wink, a nod and little said.

I saw it done by Priest and Nun,
All walks of life were there,
And not a soul near a customs patrol
Had a single thing to declare.

But worst of all in this cross-border haul,
Who smuggled through many a ton,
Was a Bishop's wife (for most of her life)
And General Montgomery's mum.

Lady Montgomery lived in Moville and travelled to Derry frequently
with a huge tin box, on which sat her Manx cat. Everybody knew that
the trunk contained contraband but no customs officer dared to touch it.

I unwisely told this story to A British Army Commissions Board
and was failed for 'Lack of social conscience'.

Socks

SOCKS are so friendly
And cosy and neat.
They really look lovely
　When placed on your feet.

You buy them in pairs
　Like peas in a pod.
They then seem so normal
　And not a bit odd.

Some people wear black,
　Whilst others like white.
The young like them coloured,
　All jazzy and bright.

There once was a craze,
　In the US of A
To be preppy and sockless,
　For most of the day.

There are men who wear socks,
　For weeks without end,
'Till the poor things are awful
　And nobody's friend.

But I like to wear mine,
　So they match pants and shoes.
A joy in the morning
　Is which ones to choose.

Sometimes they have holes,
　Which need a good darn.
For my wife to do this
　Would do her no harm.

But socks have a dark side
  And not just their colour,
That drives strong men crazy
  And wives to their mother.

"Why is it," I ask,
  "When you wash the paired things,
Some just disappear,
  As if they have wings?"

My drawers are quite full
  Of socks washed and dried,
But none of them match,
  Though I've tried and I've tried.

When socks are brand new,
  Their sight brings elation,
But wash them and dry them
  And scream with frustration.

There must be a genie,
  From soap to arise,
To make socks in water
  Change colour and size.

Man may fly to the moon,
  Tame wonders on earth,
But he cannot stop socks
  From changing their girth.

For socks are not settled,
  Like husbands and wives,
They wish to be single
  For most of their lives.

I handed a copy of this epic to a member of my household who was
moved enough to spend three hours with my socks She eventually
assembled 32 pairs.

Elk Horns

OH Irish Elk I really wish,
  You had not been a tasty dish,
For ancient men of Fir and bog,
  Who ate and chased you through the fog.

The mists of time have now revealed,
  Your horns removed, your skin well peeled,
Your remnants piled and quite discarded,
  In shed scholastic – Bursar guarded.

However, Thompson family true,
  Would like to rescue Elk Horns two.
And take them over land and brook,
  Hung high on wall for us to look.

So thinking of the fund that needs,
  A lot of cash (on which it feeds),
We offer pounds full twenty-five,
  To keep the needy fund alive.

However, if this does not bring,
  A smile of joy, a touch of spring,
To move the heart of Bursar tough,
  Who may not think we pay enough,

He can but think our future seedy,
  When school fees paid mean parents needy.
The moral of this tale sublime,
  Is each to its value in its time.

Written to the College of St Columba: my daughter Rosalind was the
first girl to enrol in my old school and one day she found the Elk horns
in a shed and it was she who started the negotiations for their purchase.
When all else failed it was decided to try the 'poem system'...
    The Bursar replied with a much better poem and accepted the offer
of £25 for the horns which now hang in Cloghan Castle.

B.D. THOMPSON

Tea with Complications in 1973

O^N the slope of a Dublin mountain in a College
    rather fine,
There dwelt an ancient bursar who made the elk horns
    mine.
So feeling rather kindly, with lashings of good will,
We took him out to dinner and saw he had his fill.

So in reciprocation, one savage wintry night,
He decided to be generous and us to tea invite.
Alas, alack, the plans of men and mice oft gang aglae,
For when he sent his card by Caird the message went
    astray.

That very Sunday evening there was a great assembly,
When up bounced Major Thompson, moustaches big
    and trembly,
"I really am most gratified and pleased as pleased can be,
That you the noble Bursar have asked us out for tea."

Surveying this utter stranger in mounting desperation,
The wily Bursar recognised a tricky situation...
"Delighted all to have you," (his brain began to
    twitch)...
"When my wife returns from England in nineteen
    seventy-six."

Now he has learned a lesson as simple as can be,
That when you meet a Thompson you can't have him
    there for tea.
Apart from table manners, which you'll really quite
    deplore,
The other one may come instead and that could be a
    bore.

Brian Thompson (major)'s Major is his dad you see,
Whilst Henry Thompson (minor) has really only me.
When I was Thompson (minor), yes –
    Thompson Brian D.
My dad was Major Thompson like the one he'll have to
    tea.

The moral of this dreadful tale
    Of woe and discontent,
Is not what is or has to be
    But what was really meant.

Brian D. Thompson: formerly Thompson (minor) son of Major Henry
Thompson and father of Henry Thompson (minor).
    Henry Thompson's (major) was a Brian Thompson whose father just
happened to be a Major Henry Thompson, (no relation), who never got
his tea.

—This was never going to be easy—

Curtains

THE purpose of curtains, or so I am told,
Is enhance, make private and keep out the cold.
Some people like curtains and treat them with pride,
Whilst others regard them as something to slide.

I hate to complain for it makes me seem glum,
But yours my dear tenant look 'sacks in a slum'.
No matter, I natter with truthful degree,
Seem to make you hang curtains with some
symmetry.

The secret of lace ones, you know – you have got 'em,
Is adjust from the top and not from the bottom.
It hurts my poor feelings, I have to admit,
To see you hang curtains like globules of shit.

Written to a tenant in 45 Wickham Road, Beckenham in 1988 to try to
get him to tidy the front curtains of our house. *It worked!*

Hospital

THE ward is sterile clean and bright.
The nurses all in starchy white.
The surgeons come and go like gods.
We lie in beds like peas in pods.

"Come take this medicine – drink this down,"
All cheery smiles, they never frown.
 The staff have all appointed tasks,
 Some take your blood and filled up flasks.

We urinate so what comes in,
Goes out with caution in its tin.
 Trainee doctors, bright and clean,
 All gather round the curtained screen.

The surgeon trainer looks at us,
Then turns around and us discuss.
 "This will come out – this will go in,
 We'll cut this off." He gives a grin.

Then on a trolley off we go,
Flat on our backs we're wheeled below,
 To lie in terror waiting fate,
 Trying not to defecate.

Then wallop, bang and in we zoom,
Right to the operating room.
 I often think that this is where,
 You learn the meaning of despair.

My guts are dealt with and I find,
I really have not lost my mind.
  If future life holds hit and miss,
  I pray it steers me miles from this.

I love you nurses as you roam,
To get us well and clean and *home*.
  But I do hope when I go away,
  That I won't come back another day.

So raise your glasses, lads, we'll drink
To those who helped us from the brink.
  We will give praise with all our heart,
  For medics are a race apart.

Written for the nurses on my departure from the Mater Hospital Dublin
June 1995.

Ascendancy

WHERE are you now old Colonel dear?
　Your times are gone afar.
Game trophies hang not in your hall,
　But Kelly's four ale bar.

The walled desmene around your home,
　Is quite the modern spread.
With little Land Commission farms,
　Where once your horses bred.

Your Georgian house from which you ruled
　Us like a great effendi,
Is gone alas to be replaced
　By brand new Haciendi.

Your servants all are grannies now,
　They dress in silk and furs.
You'd be amazed to see their cars,
　They bred entrepreneurs.

Their houses new with central heat
　Are quite a sight to see.
With vibrant colours on the walls
　And miles of carpetry.

Poor Dev's old dream of country mums
　Beside the cottage door,
Has been replaced with modern wealth
　And all they want is more.

The TV screams, loud speakers roar
　With sounds of jazz and rock.
The wardrobes creak with stylish clothes,
　The posh imbibe their Hock.

Where are you now old Colonel dear,
  Are you in heaven or hell?
The nightly chipper near your grave,
  Emits both noise and smell.

I often wonder Colonel dear,
  If uncle was quite right,
When in a haze of booze and funk
  He set your house alight.

"'Twas for the cause," he used to say,
  With logic quite erratic.
He did not wish us all to see,
  He once was a fanatic.

The Prods he said had got it wrong,
  Their accents clipped and snooty,
But I went to their church last week,
  On civic burial duty.

The Pope has said no Latin now,
  And I have thought for hours,
'Why is it then, oh Uncle Sean,
  Their service is like ours?'

I walk in Dublin suburbs now
  And I look up and down.
It is the same as Birmingham
  Or any British town.

Our rebels then are patriots now,
  Dynastic rules to pass,
The lads with guns up in the North
  Are future upper class.

You saw it then, old army man,
  As killers ran amok,
We saw it then as freedom's way
  And wished them all the luck.

Your nephew now holds open house,
 To Fine Gael he's cleft.
He charges us and shows us round
 The only mansion left.

When will we learn, as you failed too,
 When back from Hindustan,
You weren't *all* Prod and Anglicised
 You were an Irishman.

Written June 1984.
Inspired by a mobile 'chipper' beside a graveyard in Blessington.

B.D. THOMPSON

Mother Tongue

WHEN freedom came to the land of the Gael
They sent for men beyond the Pale.
A firm intention they did form,
To bring us Irish as our norm.

These men in plus fours, decked in tweed,
Were purists of a sombre breed.
 They toiled and slaved from Muff to Cork,
 Before unveiling new 'Gael talk'.

No longer could the Gents ignore
They were in peril in Mna.
 It soon came crystal clear to us
 The danger if you hailed a 'bus.

The names we knew had gone away,
The ancient ones were here to stay.
 So if them *all* you did not know
 You could not tell where you were to go.

He really was true genius born,
Who put the arse in Uctarain.
 It surely brings some slight derision,
 That telefis is television.

Aer Lingus often takes us high,
Green bird soaring in a cloudless sky.
 As up we go serene exalted
 With perfect flying never faulted.

Our hostess is a charming girl,
Who straps us in our seat.
 In *Irish* she explains to us
 The perils we might meet.

Oh utter consternation,
You poor chap from Japan,
  As safety codes in Irish,
  Confront the travelling man.

I've been around the world a bit,
And heard a thing or two,
  But nothing can compare at all,
  With Irish old and new.

The accents change and then a word
Appears by theory quite absurd.
  This vision of a promised land
  Is out of touch and out of hand.

I'm going mad in this purist's delight,
But some think it queer as well they might,
  That those who speak Irish in Donegal,
  Can't understand what they say at all.

When tourists go to Nenagh,
For B and B to stay.
  With street names all in Irish,
  They cannot find their way.

Whilst *they* are lost in Nenagh,
For reasons quite perverse,
  We all are lost in 'fairy land',
  Our culture in reverse.

Written after a trip to the Aran Island where the language was lyrical
and spoken beautifully.
    The former Vice-regal Lodge became a presidential palace and was
renamed 'Áras an Uctaráin'.

What now Oh Master?

WHAT is there to life when you have achieved,
The height of ambition, the planting of seed.
The reaping of virtue, the sum of desires,
Past dreams you have chased have been met and been
    won
Whilst rewards, once sought after, are like the fires
Which kindled in morning and flamed in the sun,
Are embers in evening – just simmering logs,
Which still throw out warmness whilst life in the
    clogs.

The answer – oh seeker – is there in the mind,
'Tis a wisdom, a knowledge and sight for the blind.
'Tis a joy and awakening to life yet unseen,
Where the rich in just money are beggars unclean.
For you see foolish fellow with questioning frown,
'Twas the game not the winning that won the best crown.
It's the effort, the trying, the striving, the pain,
That turns dross to greatness again and again.

So when you've achieved the goal you had set,
You just start all over the next goal to get.
For though you are wiser and sadder and old,
The next goal you aim for may turn out pure gold.

Freedom Mantra

I am a free man.
I will to be free.
My mind is my own.
I express my own thoughts.
I seek the truth in all things.
I reject the lies and prejudices of others.
I wish to improve myself.
I wish to improve the lot of mankind.
I will choose my own path to god.
I will choose wise leadership in all things.

I will always try to remember what freedom really means. I will always strive to attain it.

B.D. THOMPSON

I Cannot be Bothered to Vote

I am a white man I'm happy and free.
My Council house rented to me.
  My shiny new car.
  Just gleams from afar.
I've my pools, I've my fags and TV.

I am a white man, I'm happy I'm willing,
To earn me a crust or a shilling.
  As long as the work,
  Allows me to shirk,
To cheat and to strike and go killing.

I am a white man, I'm happy and good,
I confessed and was cleansed as I should,
  I do not know when
  I'll do it again.
But the priest says come back if I should.

I am a white man, I'm happy like jelly,
All I think of is sex and my belly,
  I like a good time
  And everything's fine,
If they let me drink beer and watch telly.

I am a white man, I'm happy and thick,
I know you will pay when I'm sick,
  Take from those who will work,
  Give to those who will shirk,
And the mugs will end up in the Nick.

....

I am a white man, I'm sad and effete,
I've fallen for lies and deceit.
   My freedom is shorn.
   My goodies are worn.
I've no brains, I've no gumption, I'm meat.

I may be a white man but I'm a bad case,
This Gulag is not a nice place.
   Life was too easy.
   The palms were too greasy.
False freedom is just a disgrace.

B.D. THOMPSON

The Ferry

THE young today are on the dole,
A job in Ireland is their goal.
They go to discos, talk and drink.
Their elders are just fools they think.

But I remember years ago,
When fate decreed that I must go.
No job for me on Ireland's shore,
I went the way of millions more.

To be a soldier of the King,
Was hailed as such a splendid thing.
A uniform, some pay and food,
With prospects of promotion good.

With half a pound from father got,
With travel warrant to Aldershot,
A nervous lad in a fawn raincoat,
Third class travel on the Liverpool boat.

The years went by and so did I,
A Queen now on her throne.
For all she ever thought of me,
I might have been alone.

The pay was poor, the life was hard,
I had no love for Cockney rule.
I longed for Ireland's peace and mists
The chats with friends from school.

You cannot know what it was like,
From Belfast, Cork or Derry,
Until you had the rotten luck
To travel on that ferry.

Foul festered air, tobacco smoke,
　No room to swing a finger.
The drunk all sick, Taff, Jock and Mick,
　How grim the memories linger.

The crowded train, rough khaki cloth,
　And boots with studded steel.
A hard wood floor on which to snore
　And a railway's stodgy meal.

You do not know young modern Miss,
As jetting in the sky you hiss,
　That once we travelled hard and slow,
　When the night boat train was the way to go.

Send Paddy back to his little shack,
　To his distant country home.
He went hard tack, with comfort lack,
　On a heaving wind-swept foam.

The Irish sea may seem calm to thee,
　As you twinkle your toes in Bray.
It's a pain in the neck on a heaving deck,
　On the ferry that takes you away.

With stomach gone in a crowded throng,
　On a crossing conceived in hell,
I said I'd contrive, if I stayed alive,
　To stay home for a long long spell.

I left the Queen for this land of green,
　To live within thick stone walls.
So keep me away from the salt sea spray,
　Till the final ferry calls.

Written by Brian Donovan Thompson on a dark and stormy night.

Catherine B.

THE object of railway travel,
  As far as I can see,
Is with utmost of convenience
  Try to move from A to B.

Not so when Catherine travels,
  From Dublin to her home,
For she prefers to deviate,
  Move forward back and roam.

She listens to her mother,
  Who hasn't got a clue,
And based on total ignorance,
  Instructs her what to do.

The result is total chaos,
  Which means I have to peer,
In every bloody station,
  From here to Dromineer.

Next time she takes to travel,
  Poor Catherine will have learned,
Not to listen to her mother,
  For this poor worm has turned.

No more will Thompson travel,
  Just fuming with frustration,
To look for poor lost Catherine,
  Who doesn't know her station.

PS.

The years have passed and now at last,
　　She knows where she must go,
But life is not so simple,
　　It changes to and 'fro.

She studies her timetable,
　　Her knowledge it is great,
She goes to the right station,
　　But always gets there late.

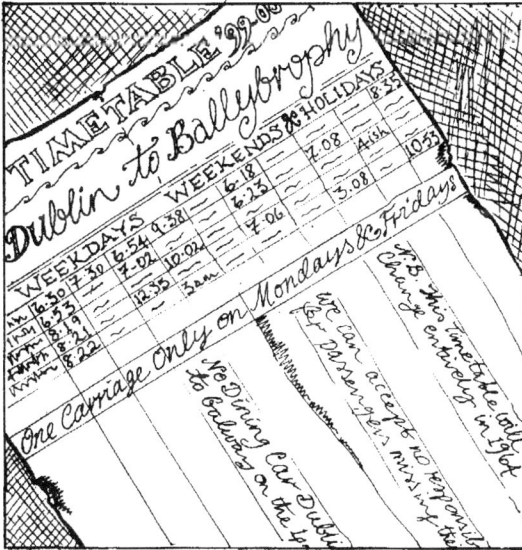

Written by an expert on meeting trains which do not contain Catherine, my step-daughter, and taking Catherine to trains which do not exist.

B.D. THOMPSON

Lament of a Dying Soldier

AWAY in the Scottish Highlands,
  In a lonely little glen,
There's a whitewashed little cabin,
  That I'll never see again.

There's a clean and sparkling river,
  Running past the cabin door,
There's my wife and there's my children,
  Who I'll see and love no more.

There's the worn old family bible,
  That my mother read at night,
There's a peace up in those mountains,
  Which would make one hate to fight.

There's a loveliness and splendour,
  Of a clear-aired Scottish dawn,
But I'll not die in Scotland,
  The land where I was born.

Written in 1945, when aged thirteen and just after my uncle, Pilot Officer George Shaw of the Royal Canadian Air Force, was killed and not long after my own father was wounded during the invasion of Europe.

Musings in the Mind of a Dynamic Sea Captain—or Bugger this Lugger, I'm Pissed with this Mist

MY whiskers white and frozen,
  But not because I'm old—
It's freezing fog on my hoary mog,
  I'm cold, I'm cold, I'm cold.

This vessel's slowly filling,
  With tons and tons of cod,
As nets are hoisted on the deck,
  By Zekeil, Sam and Todd.

I do not like the smell of fish,
  The sea is not romantic,
I'd rather face a firing squad,
  Than sail the broad Atlantic.

If I'm to be a mariner
  And I'm to be afloat,
A Mississippi paddle ship
  Is just my kind of boat.

I sit in church on Sundays,
  Bolt upright in my pew,
But I'd rather risk damnation
  With Chastity or Pru.

But now I'm on the briney,
  With it's damp and fishy smell,
This is no earthly paradise,
  It's my idea of hell.

I should have been a farmer,
  With horse and plough and harrow.
I'd even face an Indian
  With lethal bow and arrow.

New England is a healthy place,
  All godly spick and span.
But I do pine for a warmer clime
  And go there as fast as I can.

I once went down to Boston,
  In that steam engine train.
But the place was full of Methodists,
  So I won't go there again.

From whale and cod and icebergs,
  It's time to make a move,
For he who hesitates is lost,
  As life will often prove.

I'll buy a covered wagon,
  With rifle I will go,
To cross the open prairie
  And shoot the Buffalo.

I'd like to be corrupted,
  In a bar in lush Savannah,
With a lady of charm on either arm,
  In a genteel southern manner.

I'd like to pick an olive,
  From my own olive tree.
Have a life of self-indulgence,
  With no adversity.

Yes I will make a move soon,
 I will delay no more,
I'll drink my rum and have some fun.
 I'm only eighty-four.

This 'epic' was inspired one bitterly cold winter night in Newport, Rhode Island, U.S.A. as I walked down a narrow lane towards the dockside.

Written on behalf of Captain Jeremiah Benbow.

The Bed

I bought the thing in County Kent,
   Full fifteen years ago.
Its polish shone, it looked so strong,
   With age it seemed to glow.

The dealer's own, she said with pride,
   She slept in it for years.
Its parting seemed to her so sad,
   She barely held back tears.

In Surrey then I lived myself,
   In Manor old and bent,
But when this fine oak bed arrived,
   To U.S.A. it went.

It was assembled with great care,
   In Newburgh in New York.
It moved three times to different homes—
   The bed we felt could walk.

But not content with river views,
   Across the Hudson mighty,
The bed rose up and moved again,
   Its reputation flighty.

Another year of discontent,
   The bed became a hassle.
So back it fled the ocean blue,
   To live in Cloghan Castle.

A further year then with a sigh,
　As if becoming wary,
The poor old bed, all honour shed,
　Went off to Tipperary.

Alas alack one day came by—
　The experts on antique—
So off to England's auction house,
　The bed went in a week.

Rejected by the dealers there,
　Who would not buy its charm,
The bed was sent to Ulster,
　To live beside a farm.

Three years went past and then at last,
　They found it in a shed
And Thompson got a letter—
　'Pick up your bloody bed.'

So off to auction once again,
　Where not a soul would buy,
The bed returned to Comber,
　The fat began to fry.

"Take up thy bed," our William said,
　"It's like old Marco Polo,
It travels round, no buyer found,
　The lowest of the low low."

So back to Dublin I did go,
　To speak with charming Nessie.
"We'll move the bed back home at once—
　This thing's becoming messy."

The firm from Bray then went away,
  To get the bed at dawn.
But when they got there double quick,
  The flaming thing had gone.

So don't despair, we will get there
  And poster bed regain.
It won't be long till we move on
  And shift the bed again.

This travelling bed, it must be said,
  Is like a game of chance,
To sleep in it requires true grit,
  You might wake up in France.

This bed returned to Cloghan Castle and is still there chained up in the top bedroom.

Ode to a Sweetie Paper

OH how I love you, wrapping dear,
  As on my lawns with bags,
You so adorn the grass and trees,
  Like little fairy flags.

You were so sweet and charming too,
  When, round the candy sticky,
You made it easy for a child
  To make it soft and licky.

But now I stand with gaze forlorn,
  I feel aghast – disgruntled,
For there beside you littered too,
  Are thousands of you – crumpled.

You rustle over paths and flowers,
  You blow so in the breeze.
The car park overflows with you
  In heaps up to our knees.

Oh, how I wish that all the kids
  With fathers when they come,
Would pick the flaming papers up
  And take them home to Mum.

I do not want your paper cups,
  Nor glass nor polystyrene.
I do not want the butts of fags,
  Squashed flat upon my tiling.

I only hope, I only wish,
  That people kind and thoughtful,
Would tan the rears of careless mites,
  With litter habits awful.

I like my visitors to come,
  I like the weather sunny,
But when the sweetie papers fall,
  It isn't very funny.

So come now all you darling ones,
  As round my place you thunder.
Cast not a single bit of waste
  Lest you be torn asunder.

In 1966 I purchased, restored and opened to the public beautiful Putten-
den Manor, near Lingfield in Surrey. Puttenden was built in 1477 and
was a forty-roomed oak-beamed manor house of great charm, set in
thirteen acres of lawns, flowers and little lakes.

When I rented out the old stables as a tea room we began to be
plagued with ice cream papers and great quantities of other litter.

This poem on my welcoming leaflet caused many strange looks
from fathers but it *was* most effective.

Why Oh Why P. Mordecai Must I in Finance Fry?

16 *Albemarle Road*
Beckenham
Kent

3rd May 1973

To:- Collector of Taxes,
Cardiff.

Dear Sir,

Today it rained, 'twas very wet.
The wind did howl and thunder threat.
A letter came from mortgagor,
To up the interest rating more.
So on this fateful morn – it's true,
My howls of woe just grew and grew,
As tenants' cheques began to bounce,
Whilst I on diet – food renounce.
My misery is deep – forlorn.
Your letter came cold, damp and torn.
But not as torn as my poor head,
When I had read what you had said.

It's fair perhaps that I owe loot,
To tax collectors so astute,
But have a heart and have a care,
I cannot pay what is not there.

So please be patient with your loss,
If cheque – post-dated – comes across.
Please do not *do not* rouse great fears,
With interest charges on arrears.
I crave your mercy down in Wales,
Or I'll go bankrupt to your jails.

Yours faithfully,

[signature: Brian Donovan Thompson]

B.D. THOMPSON.

They granted me a slight reprieve.

Nobody Brainwashed Me

THE adman told us buy his wares.
We'll all stay young and lose no hairs.
  His promises have us enthralled,
  For "Hope of love" his product's called.
With phallic symbols fair and fine,
We know it's true right down the line.

We buy it now and buy it big,
We pay our dough, discard the wig,
  For now the arts of kind big brother
  Replace our dad, replace our mother.
Our mouths ajar in dazed delight,
We buy by day and spend by night.

I wish you could admire our sense,
As lovingly we spend our pence.
  We know it's done for our own selves,
  That hair restorer fills our shelves.

Alas one day our cash is gone,
The salesman's sad, his face is wan.
  At last he tells us quite appalled
  That *he* is old and *he* is bald.

B.D. THOMPSON

The Cultural Revolution

The sayings of Karl Marx and Mao
Are guiding the Communists now.
  Like puppets on strings,
  Or birds without wings,
The masses are chained to the plough.

Workers' Republic

The kindness of dear Uncle Joe,
Killed millions of Russians you know.
  The rulers today are really OK.
The wall of Berlin's just for show.

(These two poems were written in the nineteen sixties.)

Female Teenager in 1999

I'VE a stud in my nose and anything goes,
As a group you would scream to have seen us.
But here's a fine thought to make mother distraught,
  My boyfriend has one on his penis.

By a disadvantaged young person:
    Written after we had watched a very explicit TV documentary on
the subject.

An Italian Mystery

A person telephoned

SHE said she was a Principessa,
Not just a simple Earl's Contessa.
She came to Ireland to have tea,
In Castle Birr in Offaly.

The Earl refused with "Not this week,"
So she stamped her feet in a fit of pique.
"You ain't no kith of mine," quote he,
"You don't appear on the family tree."

"I am a cousin – have no fears,
I've been in India sixteen years."
When disbelief on her was shed,
"I'll buy a Castle then," she said.

Her Secretary called us and he spoke,
A cultured lad, not common folk.
"For twenty years with her I've been,"
A little odd, he sounds sixteen.

So nothing daunted, in good taste,
To buy our castle she made haste,
When asked to talk – and here I quote –
"I can't, a door has hit my throat."

Alas alack the telephone,
Just kept her busy all alone.
  She never reached the Thompson's door
  And disappeared for ever more.

So maybe one day in great hordes,
Will come Italians bearing boards
  Proclaiming gaily – banners high,
  "Our Principessa was a guy."

This very strange story is actually true and left all concerned very be-
wildered indeed.

Belfast Blitz

I bought a book the other day,
  In Easons in a mall.
Its pictures and its contents
  Provoked a bad recall.

In April nineteen forty,
  When I was almost eight,
I lived with loving parents
  And life was really great.

Our home it was in Belfast,
  Where they make ships and planes
And Daddy was an expert,
  Who checked the aircraft frames.

First howled the air raid sirens,
  In the middle of a night,
Then bangs and loud explosions,
  By searchlights' flickering light.

Under the kitchen table,
  All huddled with no fuss,
The roar of German bombers,
  As they rained their bombs on us.

The houses very close indeed,
  Became just heaps of trash,
And neighbours died defenceless,
  In fire and hellish crash.

They came again another night,
  Huge bombers by the score,
With docks and houses flattened,
  Along the Belfast shore.

B.D. THOMPSON

They sent me off to Derry,
  With grandpa there to stay,
My book depicts evacuees,
  My classmates – bussed away.

Another raid with firebombs,
  One landed on our home,
And father put it out with sand,
  —Unaided and alone.

Mother and I to Donegal,
  And father off to war,
We did not think we'd meet again,
  Those heartaches they were sore.

Boarding at school in Derry,
  Bullied in misery,
Streets awash with sailors,
  Back from the cruel sea.

So many girls with nylons,
  Displaying charm and thanks,
A lot of kids in Derry,
  Had fathers who were Yanks.

A general with his batman
  And officers in blue,
Billeted with Grandpa,
  Their numbers grew and grew.

When father joined the Army,
  To fight for King and Queen,
A man of rank, an officer,
  All dressed in Khaki green.

The very day that he joined up
  And left to go to fight,
A landmine fell on Belfast,
  Where he had worked at night.

It blew apart the factory
  And killed those men inside.
If he'd not joined the Army,
  That night he would have died.

A shattered saddened childhood,
  When I was very young,
But I, compared to many
  Was quite the lucky one.

Young Felix in my dorm (a Jew),
  Escaped from Prague entrained.
His people gassed by Nazis,
  Six million killed and maimed.

I read my book and tremble,
  With nightmares flooding back.
I hate the very thought of war,
  Of bombs, of death and flack.

We lived between the Shore and Antrim roads. It was one of the most heavily bombed areas in the City of Belfast.

When the anti aircraft guns fired at the enemy planes, the shells exploded in mid air and shrapnel rained down on us. It littered the streets and tore holes in the roofs of houses. Flack was the term for the 'welcoming' barrage that the gunners directed at the planes.

B.D. THOMPSON

Donovan's Bug

The Dreaded Fever of Cuddapah

THERE once was a Doctor in US of A.
Who saw in young Henry his 'laugh for the day'
    When Henry said: "Uncle to India went
    To cure vile disease and experiment."

The Doctor said, "Yes – I have heard of his fame,
He discovered the pox, a most virulent strain."
    So Henry retreated embarrassed you see,
    To think great-great uncle invented V.D.

In that part of Madras, once malodorous swamp,
Lived a bug quite revolting with slithering stomp,
    It sucked all your blood until it turned red,
    It made you so ill that you ended up dead.

As sicker and sicker you finally grew,
This smelly bug creature made supper of you.
    It gave you disease of a herpi-type strain
    So if you survived you'd have it again.

Confined to a place which is hot and quite damp,
This bug had the *hots* for the soldiers in camp.
    'Till up came old uncle with microscope steady,
    To isolate, cure and advance at the ready.

Our uncle, a Colonel, with pride he does fill us,
For he found the bug now called his Bacillus.
> It wasn't a pox of the sort soldiers earn,
> But a bug that ate blood and gave death in
> return.

Now, if you go East – to follow the sun
And perchance feel weird with a pain in your tum,
> Your life may be saved from the cure in a jar,
> Thanks to uncle – the hero of old Kal-ah-zar.

The Avenging Donovans

Written in April 1987:

Lt Col Charles Donovan MD was in the Indian Medical Service for many years. His soldiering was done with the Gurkhas on the North-West Frontier. His first civilian practice contained over one million men, women and children.

He founded the medical section of Madras University and a hospital wing is now named after him in India.

He discovered the 'Donovan Bacillus'.

B.D. THOMPSON

What is an Irishman?

IF you are to be one,
  You have to pass the test,
The length of time you've lived here
  Is good but not the best.

Your parents being Irish,
  Will help to put you right,
But that is not conclusive,
  It's *nearly* but not *quite*.

Were ancestors all Irish,
  For thousands of our years?
Did they weep for good old Ireland,
  In this land of vales and tears?

Were they rebels against England?
  Did they fight Boyne River fray?
Did they lose to *bad* King William
  And have to run away?

Did you ever learn sweet Irish,
  As you slaved away at school?
Have you mastered all the accents,
  From Kerry to Drumgool?

Did you ever take to Guinness,
  Or have you signed the pledge?
Have you seen the cliffs of Moher?
  And stood right at the edge?

Have you mastered Irish dancing,
  Or learned a song or two?
Have you eaten the potato,
  From which our sufferings grew?

Are you Irish when in England,
  And in Amerikay,
Are you Irish in all other lands,
  When you are far away?

Now if you've passed these tests, my lad,
  You're a bit of the old sod,
Unless, of course, one little thing,
  UNLESS YOU ARE A PROD.

In all fairness, we Protestants have brought this sorry state of affairs upon ourselves.

Many Protestants treated Catholics badly for centuries and we can hardly complain if we get some of this inherited unpleasantness back.

One million Irish Protestants do not wish to be Irish in the North and nearly half a million Protestants in the south have fled since independence or have been absorbed through intermarriage, when they were forced to bring up their children as Roman Catholics. Hopefully more and more people are realising that we are all the same race.

B.D. THOMPSON

Kelly the Boy from Killann

NEW York New York is a wonderful town,
Deserving rightly world renown.
The lofty buildings skywards soar,
I never saw it's like before.

Some years ago I went to see,
The home of the brave the land of the free.
So I moved house and goods and heart.
It was a fresh and different start.

The summer heat was hard to bear,
The winter cold beyond belief.
I cannot tell you how I felt,
When Spring and Autumn brought relief.

I loved their vibrant forceful life,
That driving wish to win and win.
Their open minds to different views,
From blacks and whites, Gentiles and Jews.

But times there were in inner sight,
When love of Ireland would take flight.
I'd long for greeny misty vales.
Old men in pubs who spin tall tales.

Church bells ringing on a Sunday dawn,
Eggs and bacon, chats with Sean.
Driving slow on the left hand side,
Down leafy lanes just ten feet wide.

The donkeys, dogs and smell of turf.
The waves from strangers 'fine soft day'.
  When would those memories fade away
  Of fish fresh caught out in the bay?

But then one day like a streak of light,
  That flashes in the dark,
I had a moment quite sublime
  Not far from Central Park.

A weekend morn on an empty street,
  On a misty rainy sidewalk.
Skyscrapers loom in deepening gloom,
  Soft muted was our talk.

My darling wife on my right hand side,
  As we stepped from our breakfast meal.
As we hurried along there burst a song
  Which made my senses reel.

There hunched on the road with his shoulders bowed,
  To keep out the wind and the rain,
Sang a voice so clear that all could hear,
  It was 'Kelly the boy from Killann'.

He was home that young man
You could see his thoughts ran,
  To the land of mist and the fogs,
Yes 'Kelly' like me
Had his mind running free
  He was back on those gentle soft bogs.

With tears in my eyes and a lump in my throat,
  How grateful I was for his song.
As long as I live, there's nothing to give,
  Like 'Kelly the boy from Killann'.

The original 'Kelly the boy from Killann' was a ballad inspired by a
hero of the 1798 Rebellion, Who was, incidentally, a Church of Ireland
Churchwarden from Killann.

I recently discovered why my mother's family, the Shaws of Bally-
nahinch and Saintfield, County Down were rather coy about family
history

Three 'Colonels' of the Presbyterian rebel force which won the bat-
tle of Saintfield in 1798 were Shaws. They very narrowly escaped being
hanged when the rebellion was put down.

Know it Now

Ode to a modern dictator

YOU are so smug oh thug supreme,
  To think love sham and god a dream[1]
Your stubby fingers, beetle brow,
Confine your brains I will allow.
But why must you of all mankind,
Presume to rule, enslave and bind.
You little knew and had not thought
When you seized power what you had bought.
You come to tell us all what's what,
Mouthe puerile wit best left forgot.
But when you – scum – have said your fill,
Your wild crazed eyes and lust to kill,
I know that though you rule us now
Will come a time, I know not how,
When rats like you and other vermin
Will lose your stolen gold and ermine
And facing retribution fair,
Will say to god in judgement there
You'll say as Scotsmen tell it true,
"I didna' ken lord" – "Ken the noo."

Based on a very long Presbyterian sermon.
  "I didna' ken lord," cried the sinner from the fires of hell and the
good lord in his infinite mercy gazed down and said, "Well ye ken the
noo." You know it now.

B.D. THOMPSON

For Elyse – The Girl in Blue

Now that I am growing old,
My hair is white and grey.
I'd like to let some others know
What happened far away.

She was a woman young and fair,
With body slim and shapely.
The loveliest thing I ever saw,
Or ever will again.

Then suddenly I was in love.
A thunderbolt had landed.
When nothing else was worth a damn,
My whole world it commanded.

We walked together New York streets,
Strangers stopped to stare.
They smiled and wished us 'lots of luck',
We seemed to walk on air.

I took her to the Plaza
For strawberries and cream.
The orchestra just played for us,
It now seems like a dream.

We dined and went to see a play
And walked the famous Broadway.
In silk blue dress she glowed like gold
There was no need for it be told,
'This couple were in love'.

We passed a Grecian tavern,
Men standing at the bar.
  As we came by
  Their glasses high,
They toasted 'To your life'.

You've seen it all in movies,
  And think it could not be.
But let me tell you here and now.
  It happened once to me.

Yes – truly I have been in love
  And I have known it's spell.
It's memory lingers on with me,
  It's heaven and it's hell.

I do not now regret it,
  Such moments they are few,
The greatest thing in all my life,
  That gorgeous girl in blue.

Twenty years on…

B.D. THOMPSON

The Parachutist

THE engine came to life and roared,
  We climbed aboard the plane,
We fastened up our safety belts,
  Our stomachs dulled with pain.

The chaps I knew, they all were there,
  Their faces grim and set,
Then someone laughed and shouted out,
  "Cheer up – you're not dead – yet."

The aircraft gathered speed and soon
  We felt it leave the ground,
The blast of air passed open doors
  Gave out a high pitched sound.

The orders came 'Hook up your chute,
  Fit your equipment on'.
We then undid our safety belts
  And knew we'd soon be gone.

The sticks stood up and checked their kit,
  Then shouted out "All right".
We moved up close beside the doors
  And waited for the light.

The red light on 'Stand in the door'
  Then glittered on the green,
And singly out the doors we sprang
  To hit the strong slipstream.

The terror of it haunts me still,
    As I recall my flight,
My palms from dry go cold and wet,
    My horror and my fright.

I twisted in the air and thought,
    My life would soon be done,
Then suddenly I felt a jerk
    And out in space I hung.

Suspended by my chute I swayed,
    For seconds thirty-five,
Then crash – I landed on the ground,
    Bruised , jolted but alive.

I sang, I laughed, I yelled with joy,
    I sneered at death and pain.
I'd feel a brave and fearless man
    Until I jumped again.

B.D.T. 1953.
Seventeen jumps with no reserve chute.

B.D. THOMPSON

The Drive-In Movie

THEY all went to a movie,
  In Florida's clear night air.
The three of them in a Buick,
  For Rogers and dancing Astaire.

Bill's pal he was no looker,
  Nor was his homely spouse.
For Freddie was touching forty,
  And built like a red brick house.

Bill's sense of good direction,
  Was not too finely honed.
Though later he'd have a bypass,
  He was slim and quite lightly boned.

"I'll go and get the popcorn,"
  It was Bill who had volunteered.
Alas alack when returning back,
  He got lost – it was worse than he'd feared.

To car after car he went searching,
  But few were amused when he peered.
With hands clutching boxes of popcorn
  And in danger of being thought weird.

When finally he saw a Buick
  And climbed the back seat to his place,
He surprisingly saw his friend Freddie,
  In a fond and a heated embrace.

His glasses were steaming and misted
  As in enlightenment gradually grew.
He was sitting in quite the wrong Buick,
  With a couple quite totally new.

Now fearing his own swift extinction,
  He wasn't quite built for a fight.
With extreme care he opened the car door
  And crept quietly off in the night.

Of course he abandoned the popcorn,
  To sustain and surprise those he'd left,
And went crawling around in the car park,
  Not a shred of his dignity left.

When he finally reached the right Buick
  He thought back to what he had seen.
More lurid sights in the automobiles
  Than anything shown on a screen.

This happened long, long ago and besides it was in another country.

It was, however, based on a true story but the names have been
changed to protect the innocent. I often wonder what they thought when
they smelt the popcorn.

B.D. THOMPSON

To go on the North Bawn Wall of Cloghan Castle

TWO Hogans built this wall for me.
The wall behind was the work of three.
I roofed the towers and cleared the lawn,
Did Main Guard, Great Hall and the bawn.
Furnished throughout with love and care,
Antiques ancient and portraits rare.
If I came here wealthy and leave here bust.
'Twas to save the Castle when I am dust.

Finis

THE clue to my poems, if that you seek,
Is not what is said, but the tongue in the
cheek.
If you have been stirred to think and to doubt,
My task has been done to push apathy out.
For though we all fail in strength and ideals,
There is more to church bells than the ringing of peals,
There's more to a sermon than lofty text giving,
And a lot more to life than just simply living.

Cloghan Castle – North Front

Cloghan Castle – Southern Aspect

Drawn by Malcolm Ross-Macdonald

OUT OF MY SYSTEM

AN ASSORTMENT OF PITHY POEMS

written by Brian Donovan Thompson
was typeset by Richard Graham,
illustrated by Rosalind Fanning,
and printed and bound by
Antony Rowe, Chippenham, Wiltshire, England.

This edition, printed on 100gsm Arrow MF
and bound in crimson Wibalin with gold blocking,
is limited to
five hundred copies.

This book was published in May, 2000
by
BATTLEMENTS PRESS
Lusmagh, Banagher, Co Offaly, Ireland,
Brian Donovan Thompson, publisher.

Copy: ......   Signed: *Brian Donovan Thompson*